Kids Online™

A Smart Kid's Guide to

Online Bullying

David J. Jakubiak

PowerKiDS
press
New York

For my parents, who made sure I always had someone I could talk with.

Published in 2010 by The Rosen Publishing Group, Inc.
29 East 21st Street, New York, NY 10010

First Edition

Editor: Amelie von Zumbusch
Book Design: Julio Gil
Photo Researcher: Jessica Gerweck

Photo Credits: Cover © www.iStockphoto.com/Nina Shannon; p. 5 Bob Stevens/Getty Images; p. 6 © www.iStockphoto.com/Cliff Parnell; p. 9 Charlotte Nation/Getty Images; pp. 10, 13 Bruce Laurance/Getty Images; p. 14 © www.iStockphoto.com/Mark Hatfield; p. 17 Tony Anderson/Getty Images; p. 18 Matt Henry Gunther/Getty Images; p. 21 Shutterstock.com.

Library of Congress Cataloging-in-Publication Data

Jakubiak, David J.
  A smart kid's guide to online bullying / David J. Jakubiak. — 1st ed.
      p. cm. — (Kids online)
  Includes index.
  ISBN 978-1-4042-8114-1 (library binding) — ISBN 978-1-4358-3348-7 (pbk.) —
ISBN 978-1-4358-3349-4 (6-pack)
  1. Cyberbullying—Juvenile literature. I. Title.
  HV6773.J347 2010
  302.3—dc22
                                                    2009000695

Manufactured in the United States of America
CPSIA Compliance Information: Batch #CR016250PK: For Further Information Contact Rosen Publishing, New York, New York at 1-800-237-9932

Contents

What Is an Online Bully?   4

A Cyberbully in Your Inbox   7

Why Cyberbullies Bully   8

Taking Off the Mask   11

Making a Case   12

Getting Help   15

Shutting a Cyberbully Down   16

Staying Safe Online   19

Don't Be a Cyberbully   20

Safety Tips   22

Glossary   23

Index   24

Web Sites   24

What Is an Online Bully?

Bullies hurt people. Some bullies hit, slap, or kick their **targets**. These bullies can bully only in person. However, other bullies use words or pictures to scare their targets. They try to make their targets feel weak. These bullies can even bully from far away. A cyberbully is someone who sends messages on computers and telephones to spread fear.

Cyberbullies use Web sites and message boards to tell lies and act tough. For example, these bullies may put **embarrassing** pictures of their targets online to make them feel bad. Luckily, knowing how cyberbullies work can help you deal with one.

Cyberbullies use their computers to pick on other kids. If you write messages on Web sites calling your classmates dumb or ugly, you are being a cyberbully.

You may feel hurt and angry if you receive mean e-mails that make fun of your clothes or your family. Do not let cyberbullies keep you from using e-mail, though.

A Cyberbully in Your Inbox

Computers and cellular phones allow people to stay in touch. The good news is that this means your family and friends are always only a few clicks away. The bad news is that computers and cellular phones make it possible for bullies to reach their targets anywhere. Cyberbullies can even get to people in their own homes.

There are many ways that cyberbullies can try to reach you. These bullies can send an unwanted e-mail or **text message**. Cyberbullies can also post nasty notes on your Web site. A cyberbully may even write a story about you online that is not true.

Why Cyberbullies Bully

All bullies, including cyberbullies, bully for a reason. They may feel bad about themselves and may think being a bully will make them feel better. They may get bullied by someone else and think that bullying will give them power.

Cyberbullies can feel **anonymous**. They often hide behind **screen names** and stop you from seeing their phone numbers when sending text messages. Cyberbullies may pretend to be someone they are not. This makes them believe they can control what other people think. Cyberbullies often think they will not get caught. However, cyberbullies can be caught, and they sometimes get into big trouble for their bullying.

Some cyberbullies think that making fun
of other people will make their friends think that they are cool.
However, these people are really just being mean.

You can sometimes guess who is cyberbullying you from what the bully says. For example, a cyberbully who makes fun of a report you did for school is most likely in your class.

Taking Off the Mask

Getting bullied online can be especially scary if you do not know who is sending you messages. However, if you get a message from a cyberbully using a screen name, there are ways you can figure out the bully's real name.

For example, take note of the words that a cyberbully uses in a message. Bullies often use the same words in person that they use online. Sometimes the messages of bullies will talk about things that they have done in person. When you read a message from a cyberbully, ask yourself, "Does this sound like someone I know?"

Making a Case

Every message that a cyberbully sends can give you a clue in figuring out who the bully is. Cyberbullies generally send the same kind messages over and over again. Collecting these messages can give you **evidence** against a cyberbully.

You should print out and save any e-mails you have received from a cyberbully. Text messages can be forwarded to an adult's phone. You can use a **screen shot** to catch mean or scary things that a cyberbully says in a chat room or on a message board **thread**. Since a cyberbully sometimes uses several names, record the names of everyone who sends you bullying messages.

Writing a list of all the people from whom you have received cyberbullying messages is a good idea. Keeping track of the dates on which you receive these mean messages can be useful, too.

13

Talking to a trusted adult about mean messages
you have received from a cyberbully is more than just the first step in
getting help. It can also make you feel better.

Getting Help

Being targeted by a cyberbully hurts. If your inbox is full of mean messages, it can make you feel alone. When people are saying bad things about you on a Web site, it can seem as if the whole world is against you. Remember, you are not alone.

Telling a trusted adult, like a parent, guardian, or teacher, can be a huge step in stopping cyberbullying. Aunts, uncles, grandparents, and babysitters are also good people to talk to. Adults can help you collect your evidence. They can even help you figure out ways to put an end to the bullying. There are computer tools that adults can use to help uncover the name of a bully.

Shutting a Cyberbully Down

There are rules on the Internet. For example, online message boards have rules about what people can write on them. Using bad words and putting people down is often not allowed. There are rules about what people can send by e-mail, too. Web sites are **hosted** by companies called Internet service providers, or ISPs. ISPs have rules about what people can and cannot do on Web sites. Breaking the rules can get bullies kicked off sites.

If you get a bullying message, tell an adult. Adults can call or e-mail the ISP and ask the people there to deal with the problem. Always tell an adult if a cyberbully says that he or she will beat you up or hurt you. The adult may decide to tell the police.

If you have been cyberbullied, the adults in your family may want to gather evidence, look at the messages, and talk over the problem to figure out if they need to go to the police.

If a cyberbully is using text messages to get to you, tell an adult. Adults can get the phone company to block text messages from certain phone numbers or e-mail addresses.

Staying Safe Online

The best way to stop cyberbullies is to keep them from reaching you. Cyberbullies can reach you only if they know how to find you. Think carefully before giving out your phone number, your e-mail address, or your Web site. Use an **alias** for your e-mail address and screen name.

If a cyberbully sends you a message, do not reply. Cyberbullies want you to reply. Instead, **block** bullies so that they cannot reach you again. Ask an adult if you need help blocking messages from a certain e-mail address. Remember, you have done nothing wrong. It is the cyberbully who may be breaking the law.

Don't Be a Cyberbully

The targets of cyberbullies may want to bully the cyberbully back. However, this would only put another cyberbully on the Internet.

When you talk to people in person, you likely use **etiquette**. You would not yell at them, say things to scare them, or try to be tougher than them. Always remember to be respectful when talking to people online, too. Do not type in all capital letters because that is like yelling. Do not use bad words. Never send e-mails when you are angry. If you do, people may mistake you for a cyberbully. Everyone online can help stop cyberbullying. Remember this before you press "send."

If you are friendly and respectful in your e-mails, text messages, and instant messages, you are much more likely to get friendly replies.

Safety Tips

- Keep your e-mail address, instant-messaging screen name, and phone numbers private.

- Do not forward e-mails without first asking the person who wrote the e-mail.

- Only open messages from people you know and never reply to messages from a cyberbully!

- Do not post pictures of yourself online before checking with an adult.

- Never post pictures of your friends without asking them first.

- Print mean messages to show to an adult. Then block the sender, and delete the message.

- Educate your friends about cyberbullies.

- Start a Cyberbully Stoppers Club so you and your friends can talk about your experiences on the Internet.

Glossary

alias (AY-lee-us) A made-up name that someone uses to hide his or her real name.

anonymous (un-NAH-neh-mus) Unknown.

block (BLAHK) To stop or slow the actions others.

embarrassing (em-BAR-us-ing) Causing shame or uneasiness.

etiquette (EH-tih-kit) The right way to behave.

evidence (EH-vuh-dunts) Facts that prove something.

hosted (HOST-ed) Given a home.

screen names (SKREEN NAYMZ) Names people use online.

screen shot (SKREEN SHAHT) A saved copy of what shows up on a computer screen at a certain time.

targets (TAHR-gits) People who are the object of a bully's attention.

text message (TEKST MEH-sij) A written message sent by cellular phone.

thread (THRED) A chain of online messages about a subject.

Index

C
computers, 4, 7

E
etiquette, 20
evidence, 12, 15

F
family, 7
friends, 7, 22

H
homes, 7

L
lies, 4

M
message boards,
    4, 16

P
pictures, 4, 22

S
screen name(s), 8,
    11, 19, 22

screen shot, 12

T
targets, 4, 7, 20
telephones, 4, 7, 12
text message(s),
    7–8, 12
thread, 12

W
Web site(s), 4, 7,
    15–16, 19
words, 4, 11, 16, 20

Web Sites

Due to the changing nature of Internet links, PowerKids Press has developed an online list of Web sites related to the subject of this book. This site is updated regularly. Please use this link to access the list: www.powerkidslinks.com/onlin/bully/